Oh Holy Night

Oh Holy Night
The Peace of 1914

Michael C. Snow
Illustrations by *Annie Berzovan*

Printed by
Evangel Press
Nappanee, Indiana
For Orders:
1-800-253-9315

ISBN 978-1-61623-080-7
Library of Congress Control Number 2009910629

Cover photo, from the Milwaukee Soldiers Home,
a place that gave refuge and care to many veterans
of the Great War.
Copyright *Patricia A. Lynch,* Harvest Graphics,
Hales Corners, Wisconsin, USA.
Used with permission.

To

Carmen,

my bride

Peace I leave with you, my peace I give unto you: not as the world giveth, give I unto you. Let not your heart be troubled, neither let it be afraid.

Jesus the Messiah

Contents

Oh Holy Night..11

Christmas 1914: Soldiers' Letters to Home...........27

Christmas Wanes: Ending the Truces 49

The Cousins: Tragedy and Triumph 53

Armistice: The Ending of Hostilities.....................71

The End of the Beginning...................................81

Epilogue 93

Notes 95

OH HOLY NIGHT

Sometime prior to the spring of 4 B.C., before the death of King Herod the Great, an event came to pass which would come to mark the span of all time and which would wondrously affect Christmas, A.D. 1914, in the midst of what was to be named the Great War.

That event brought a peace markedly different from the fleeting Pax Romana. Marching legions wielding swords, and a conquering Caesar could not usher in such a peace. Rather, it was inaugurated by angels who heralded the birth of a child.

And there were in the same country shepherds abiding in the field, keeping watch over their flock by night.

And, lo, the angel of the Lord came upon them, and the glory of the Lord shone round about them: and they were sore afraid.
And the angel said unto them, Fear not: for, behold, I bring you good tidings of great joy, which shall be to all people.

For unto you is born this day in the city of David a Saviour, which is Christ the Lord.

And this shall be a sign unto you; Ye shall find the babe wrapped in swaddlingclothes, lying in a manger.

And suddenly there was with the angel a multitude of the heavenly host praising God, and saying,

"Glory to God in the highest, and on earth peace, good will toward men."

The Gospel of St. Luke

It was still freezing hard on Christmas Eve ... [under] bright moonlight ...

After a timeless dream I saw what looked like a large white light on top of a pale ... It was a strange sort of light ... What sort of lantern was it? I did not think much about it; it was part of the strange unreality of the silent night, of the silence of the moon, now turning a brownish yellow, of the silence of the frost mist ...

Suddenly there was a short quick cheer from the German lines – Hoch! Hoch! Hoch! With others, I flinched and crouched, ready to fling myself flat, pass the leather thong of my rifle over my head and aim to fire, but no other sound came ...

We stood up, talking about it, in little groups ... other cheers were coming across the black spaces of no man's land. We saw dim figures on the enemy parapet, about more lights; and with amazement saw that a Christmas tree was being set there, and around it Germans were talking and laughing together.

... from the German parapet, a rich baritone voice begun to sing a song I remembered from my nurse Minne singing it to me after my evening tub before bed. She had been maid to my German grandmother ...

Stille Nacht! Heil'ge Nacht!
Alles schläft, einsam wacht
Nur das traute hoch heilige Paar.
Holder Knab' im lockigen Haar.
Schlafe in himmlischer Ruh!

Stille Nacht! Heil'ge Nacht!
Gottes Sohn, o wie lacht
Lieb' aus deinem göttlichen Mund,

Da uns schlägt die rettende Stund'.
Jesus in deiner Geburt!

Silent night Holy night
All is calm all is bright
'Round yon virgin Mother and Child
Holy infant so tender and mild
Sleep in heavenly peace

Silent night, holy night,
Son of God, love's pure light.
Radiant beams from Thy holy face,
With the dawn of redeeming grace,
Jesus, Lord, at Thy birth;
Jesus, Lord, at Thy birth.

... Stille Nacht! Heilige Nacht! Tranquil Night! Holy Night! The grave and tender voice rose out of the frozen mist, it was all so strange.

... it was like being in another world, to which one had come through a nightmare; a world finer than the one I had left behind in England ...

And back again in the wood it seemed so strange that we had not been fired upon; wonderful that the mud had gone; wonderful to walk easily on the paths; to be dry; to be able to sleep again.

The wonder remained in the low golden light of a white-rimmed Christmas morning. I could hardly realise it; but my chronic, hopeless longing to be home was gone.

Private Henry Williamson,
London Rifle Brigade

This wonder burst forth on Christmas Eve, 1914, for a lad who had just turned nineteen. Here, the fields in France had been transformed into No Man's Land. But in that moment, this was now all men's land.

Private Frederick Heath, somewhere else along those 400 and some miles of the Western Front, also described it [Printed in the North Mail, January 8th 1915, found and transcribed by Marian Robson of Whickham, Newcastle-upon-Tyne]:

> The night closed in early – the ghostly shadows that haunt the trenches came to keep us company as we stood to arms. Under a pale moon, one could just see the grave-like rise of ground which marked the German trenches two hundred yards away. Fires in the English lines had died down, and only the squelch of the sodden boots in the slushy mud, the whispered orders of the officers and the NCOs, and the moan of the wind broke the silence of the night. The soldiers' Christmas Eve had come at last, and it was hardly the time or place to feel grateful for it.
>
> Memory in her shrine kept us in a trance of saddened silence. Back somewhere in England, the fires were burning in cozy rooms; in fancy I heard laughter and the thousand melodies of reunion on Christmas eve.
>
> With overcoat thick with wet mud, hands cracked and sore with the frost, I leaned against the side of the trench ... Thoughts surged madly in my mind, but they had no sequence, no cohesion. Mostly they were of home as I had known it through the years that had brought me to this.

I asked myself why I was in the trenches in misery at all.

Still looking and dreaming, my eyes caught a flare in the darkness. A light in the enemy's trenches was so rare at that hour that I passed a message down the line. I had hardly spoken when light after light sprang up along the German front. Then quite near our dug-outs, so near as to make me start and clutch my rifle, I heard a voice, there was no mistaking that voice with its guttural ring. With ears strained, I listened, and then, all down our line of trenches there came to our ears a greeting unique in war: "English soldier, English soldier, a merry Christmas, a merry Christmas!"

Following that salute boomed the invitation from those harsh voices: "Come out, English soldier; come out here to us." For some little time we were cautious, and did not answer. Officers, fearing treachery, ordered the men to be silent. But up and down our line one heard the men answering that Christmas greeting from the enemy. How could we resist wishing each other a Merry Christmas, even though we might be at each other's throats immediately afterwards? So we kept up a running conversation with the Germans, all the while our hands ready on our rifles. Blood and peace, enmity and fraternity – war's most amazing paradox. The night wore on to dawn – a night made easier by songs from the German trenches, the pipings of piccolos and from our broad lines laughter and Christmas carols. Not a shot was fired ...

Came the dawn, penciling the sky with grey and pink. Under the early light we saw our foes moving recklessly about the top of their trenches. Here, indeed, was courage ... Then came the invitation to fall out of the trenches and meet half way.

Still cautious we hung back. Not so the others. They ran forward in little groups, with hands held up above their heads, asking us to do the same. Not for long could such an appeal be resisted – beside, was not the courage up to now all on one side? Jumping up onto the parapet, a few of us advanced to meet the on-coming Germans. Out went the hands and tightened in the grip of friendship. Christmas had made the bitterest foes friends.

Here was no desire to kill, but just the wish of a few simple soldiers (and no one is quite so simple as a soldier) that on Christmas Day, at any rate, the force of fire should cease ...

Horrific events and extreme hardships preceded that holy night. Vienna had declared war on July 28th, setting in motion a sequence of battles which by early September claimed over a half million casualties for the French and Germans. The last quarter of 1914 bore ever-increasing fruits of death and carnage.

In Belgium, the Battle of Ypres claimed almost 60,000 British soldiers, 50,000 French, and 130,000 Germans, for whom it was "kindermord bei Ypern" – The Massacre of the Innocents of Ypres.

November, with heavy rain, snow and blizzards, brought that battle to an end but it could never wash away the nightmares. A Sergeant at Ypres called it "hell upon earth."

This was the world of the soldier during those months in 1914 leading up to Christmas.

They endured rain and mud for weeks, living in the presence of never-ending death. Rats and lice and gangrene accompanied them in their trenches. Cannon bursts, incessant shooting, and night flares made sleep fleeting. Alfred Anderson, a soldier of eighteen at that time, remembered it a year before his death at the age of 109. "All I'd heard for two months in the trenches was the hissing, cracking and whining of bullets in flight, machine gun fire and distant German voices."

Hands and feet were not only wet and cold but swollen ankles crippled the capacity of many soldiers. Until the freeze, everything was wet, and even then water in the trenches never ceased its numbing work. Their coats were stiff like boards as they daily slogged through what one soldier termed "the eternal mud", ankle deep or worse, while doing their duty, defending their lives, dodging artillery shells, dreaming of home.

But now, in their dark world, the light of Christmas shone.

From those of the 6th Battalion of the Gordon Highlanders, this account was given:

"At Christmas 1914 there took place in some parts of the British line what is still regarded by many as the most remarkable incident of the War – an unofficial truce. During the winter it was not unusual for little groups of men to gather in a front trench, and there hold impromptu concerts, singing patriotic songs. The Germans, too, did much the same, and on calm evenings the songs from one line floated to the trenches of the other side, and were received with applause, and sometimes with calls for an encore. On quiet nights, at points where the trenches were quite near, remarks shouted from one trench system were audible in the other. Christmas Eve the Germans spent singing carols, and, the night being calm, they informed our men they did not intend to shoot on Christmas Day, asking at the same time that we also should refrain from violence. 'No shoot to-night, Jock!, Sing to-night!' was one of the remarks they made on Christmas Eve. Little attention was given to this, but on Christmas morning, when our men were at breakfast, a cry was raised that the Germans had left their trenches. Springing to arms, they could scarcely believe their eyes when they looked over the parapet and saw a number of the enemy standing in the open in front of their trenches, all unarmed. Some of the enemy shouted 'No shoot!' and after a little, a number of our men also got out of their trench."

Meanwhile Colonel McLean had come up on his daily tour of inspection, accompanied by the Padre, the Rev J Esslemont Adams, minister of the West United Free Church, Aberdeen. They had just completed a burial service over one of our men behind the line, when the Chaplain, looking up, observed the strange sight at the front trench, and drew the Colonels attention to it. Colonel McLean ran along the front line and ordered our men to come down, but they pointed out that more of our men further along were standing "on the top", and that a number of the enemy were out on their side and gazing peacefully across. The Chaplain, who had followed the Colonel, said to him, 'I'm off, sir, to speak to the Germans; maybe we could get a truce to bury the dead in No Man's Land.' Coming to a little ditch, which ran along the middle of the field between the lines, he held up his hands and called out, 'I want to speak to your Commanding Officer. Does anyone speak English?' Several German officers were standing together, and one of them said, 'Yes, come over the ditch.' The Chaplain hurried forward, saluted the German Commander, and began to talk to him and his staff. Almost at the same moment a hare burst into view and raced along between the lines. Scots and Germans leapt from their trenches and joined in the eager chase. The hare was captured by the Germans, but more was secured than a hare. The truce of God had been called, and the rest of Christmas Day was filled with peace and goodwill."

In No Man's Land [the area between the opposing trenches], often strewn with bodies and barbed wire, car-

ols and prayers now broke forth; handshakes and hugging; the exchanging of addresses to meet after the war. Gifts and souvenirs traded hands; buttons and coins; cigars and pipes; food and drink. One captain returning from headquarters to those front lines found the trenches abandoned with hundreds of soldiers standing unarmed in that wasted land. "Scots and Huns were fraternizing in the most genuine possible manner. Every sort of souvenir was exchanged, addresses given and received, photos of families shown ..."

Several letters to home mention football being played. One diary entry records, "The English brought a soccer ball from the trenches and pretty soon a lively game ensued. How marvellously wonderful, yet how strange it was. The English officers felt the same way about it. Thus Christmas, the celebration of Love, managed to bring mortal enemies together as friends for a time."

But for others, the day remained sombre, as they buried their dead. From one sector along that front, a rifleman wrote to his wife:

"During the early part of the morning the Germans played some Christmas carols and 'God Save the King', and 'Home Sweet Home.' We took advantage of the quiet day and brought our dead in."

Amongst the Gordon Highlanders, the Chaplain had "organized a joint service in no-man's land with prayers in German and English. Both sides wrote home using phrases like 'fairy tale', 'day of fiction' and 'extraordinary.'" (Neil Griffiths, press officer, in the Edinburgh News.)

Other letters describe the day as 'incredible', 'most wonderful', and with 'wonderment' and speak of 'expecting disbelief.' [Sadly, something too common regarding the Christ of Christmas.]

One summed it up, "A strange sight, truly!"

... And it came to pass, as the angels were gone away from them into heaven, the shepherds said one to another, Let us now go even unto Bethlehem, and see this thing which is come to pass, which the Lord hath made known unto us.

And they came with haste, and found Mary, and Joseph, and the babe lying in a manger.

And when they had seen it, they made known abroad the saying which was told them concerning this child.

And all they that heard it wondered at those things which were told them by the shepherds.

But Mary kept all these things, and pondered them in her heart.

And the shepherds returned, glorifying and praising God for all the things that they had heard and seen, as it was told unto them.

"A Carol From Flanders"
Frederick John Niven (1878–1944)

In Flanders on the Christmas morn
The trenched foemen lay,
the German and the Briton born,
And it was Christmas Day.

The red sun rose on fields accurst,
The grey fog fled away;
But neither cared to fire the first,
For it was Christmas Day!

They called from each to each across
The hideous disarray,
For terrible has been their loss:
"Oh, this is Christmas Day!"

Their rifles all they set aside,
One impulse to obey;
'Twas just the men on either side,
Just men – and Christmas Day.

They dug the graves for all their dead
And over them did pray:
And Englishmen and Germans said:
"How strange a Christmas Day!"

Between the trenches then they met,
Shook hands, and e'en did play
At games on which their hearts were set
On happy Christmas Day.

Not all the emperors and kings,
Financiers and they
Who rule us could prevent these things –
For it was Christmas Day.

Oh ye who read this truthful rime
From Flanders, kneel and say:
God speed the time when every day
Shall be as Christmas Day.

Christmas 1914:
Soldiers' Letters to Home

27 December

A t last I have found the time to answer all your letters. Well dear, you asked me to let you know what kind of Christmas I had. Well I never had a merry one because we were in the trenches, but we were quite happy. Now what I am going to tell you will be hard to believe, but it is quite true. There was no firing on Christmas Day and the Germans were quite friendly with us. They even came over to our trenches and gave us cigars and cigarettes and chocolate and of course we gave them things in return. Just after one o'clock on Christmas morning I was on look-out duty and one of the Germans wished me Good morning and a Merry Christmas. I was never more surprised in my life when daylight came to see them all *sitting on top of the trenches waving their hands and singing to us. Just before we came out of the trenches (we came out of them on Christmas night) one of them shouted across, "Keep your heads down, we are just going to fire" and they sent about a dozen bullets flying over the top of our heads. Now who would believe it if they did not see it with their own eyes? It is hard enough for us to believe. What kind of Christmas did you have? I do hope you enjoyed yourself. I thought of you a good many times. I don't expect it was much of a Christmas in England. I haven't received mother's parcel yet. I wonder what has become of it. I have had some eatables but they were nowhere near as good as mother's."*

Lance Corporal Cooper

8 January

*D**ear Miss Fuller and other assistants of the little tea shop. Just a few lines to let you know how we are all keeping. The 6th have been in the trenches twice. A good few of them had to go to hospital through the cold and exposure. They are hardly fit for this work. We were in the trenches on Christmas Day. We spent a merrier day than we expected. There was a truce to bury our dead. **We had a short service over the graves, conducted by our minister and the German one. They read the 23rd Psalm** and had a short prayer. I don't think I will ever forget the Christmas Day I spent in the trenches. After the service we were speaking to the Germans and getting souvenirs from them. Fancy shaking hands with the enemy! I suppose you will hardly believe this, but it is the truth. I often think about the little tea shop* *and wonder how you are getting on. Long may the lum reek at the little tea-shop.*

Pte. B. Calder, 6th Gordons

Psalm 23

The LORD is my shepherd; I shall not want.

*He maketh me to lie down in green pastures:
he leadeth me beside the still waters.*

*He restoreth my soul: he leadeth me in the paths
of righteousness for his name's sake.*

*Yea, though I walk through the valley of the
shadow of death, I will fear no evil: for thou art
with me; thy rod and thy staff they comfort me.*

*Thou preparest a table before me in the
presence of mine enemies: thou anointest
my head with oil; my cup runneth over.*

*Surely goodness and mercy shall follow me all
the days of my life: and I will dwell in the house
of the LORD for ever.*

I am writing this to you as I have just heard that my letters posted on Dec 26th were lost. There was a breakdown with a motor lorry, which got on fire, and all letters were burnt. I was sending Princess Mary's gift and the King's and Queen's Christmas card to you. I don't know whether they were lost or not. We were in the trenches all Christmas week, and the weather was awful. On Christmas Day we had a lot of firing over us, and shells too. All at once it ceased and I looked up and saw the Germans on top of their trenches shouting to us, and asking us to meet them. All our brigade went, and we were talking to them about two hours. They asked us not to fire that day and said they would not; and no firing was done until next day and then we were fighting for all we were worth. Times however are hard here. In the trenches we are up to our waists in water with shells bursting over us and no sleep. We keep on advancing and having to retire on account of fierce shelling. We should be relieved now by Kitchener's Army. I was in the battles of La Bassee and Ypres and the retirements, and it was simply awful. My bayonet was stained more than once. I said my prayers! The Bedfords regained the trenches that other regiments had lost. They retired and we had to retire also. It was like hell upon earth. Then we rallied up and charged the Germans out of them and took a lot of prisoners, but at what a loss. When we mustered up next day we had lost about 76 in my company (A Co.). I had some marvellous escapes.

Sergeant W. Blundell

Christmas Day

*L*ast night the Germans lit up their trenches and started calling across merry Christmas. We responded in the same way and then we started singing songs to one another, carols etc. We then sang the Austrian national anthem and they responded with God Save the King after which we cheered lustily. By this time all shooting had stopped. We walked about the parapets of the trenches and called out to one another. Then some of our chaps walked out and met some of the Germans half way, wishing each other a merry Christmas, shook hands and said they would not fight today. **We had communion this morning** in a farm about half a mile away. We set out before day light to be on the safe side. It was very strange. The farm had been bombarded and consequently it was in a bad way. Where we held the service half the roof was off. I don't suppose I shall ever go to such another service – it was so reverent and the surroundings so rough ... We got back safely and then some of our chaps started kicking a football about outside the trench. Then the Germans showed themselves and to cut a long story short it finished up with us meting one another half way shaking hands exchanging fags and souvenirs and parting the best of friends. One has given me his address to write to him after the war. They were quite a decent lot of fellows I can tell you. I know this seems an unbelievable story but it is fact. I am sure if it was left to the men there would be no war.

A Gateshead soldier.

 [26] *And as they were eating, Jesus took bread, and blessed it, and brake it, and gave it to the disciples, and said, Take, eat; this is my body.*

 [27] *And he took the cup, and gave thanks, and gave it to them, saying, Drink ye all of it;*

 [28] *For this is my blood of the new testament, which is shed for many for the remission of sins.*

 [29] *But I say unto you, I will not drink henceforth of this fruit of the vine, until that day when I drink it new with you in my Father's kingdom.*

 [30] *And when they had sung an hymn, they went out into the mount of Olives.*

Matthew 26

*W*e spent Christmas Day in the trenches. Not a very warm spot but we were quite able to sing a few songs. The Germans treated us to music too. We were only 60 yards or so from them. We have now had two turns in the trenches, the first time six days and nights, the second four. The weather has been none too good or warm. On Christmas Day we had the honour of meeting and speaking with the Germans. They emerged unarmed from their trenches and soon we met halfway between our trenches and theirs. An experience of a lifetime I should think and one very rare. We have failed to fathom it yet but many of us thought there were as decent Germans as there are British.

Lance Corporal Robert Alexander

*A*bout 5pm on Thursday, when in the trenches our thought turned to home and Christmas Eve, and we started singing a few carols. This seemed to cheer the Germans as they too began to sing, and shout to us, "A Merry Christmas". Not a shot was fired by them or by us all night and it seemed as if the war had almost finished. Next day, Christmas Day, we had a short service in the trench and after that we started going halfway to meet the Germans. In less than half an hour, we were busily talking to them and found that they were eager for the war to cease. Two of them with whom I happened to get into conversation, were quite decent fellows and a cut above the others. They were brothers in the 107th Saxons and being Reservists were called up. One had a ticket for London with him and told us that he was just going to London for a holiday when he was called up. Both said they were personally very sorry to have to fight against us.

A private

I was on sentry duty just as Christmas Day arrived and I must confess that it was indeed beautiful to hear the Germans singing carols and their national anthem. We too were all singing and cheering at the pitch of our voices; it was "just like being at home"! At about four o'clock in the morning, the Germans again struck up with four or five musical instruments all of which played Christmas carols and during all the time the music was being wafted through the air you could hear a pin fall. We were entrenched a few hundred yards from the Germans and the whole affair, I must confess, seemed and felt very touching indeed. We shell and snipe at each other from morning till night, this as you will be aware causes much damage to both sides. We have lots of narrow shaves out here and several times I have been struck with shrapnel but the wounds were very slight and trifling and I trust to God that such will be the case until the finish.

Private John McKay

C hristmas in the trenches. It must have been sad do you say? Well I am not sorry to have spent it there and the recollection of it will ever be one of imperishable beauty. At midnight a baritone stood up and in a rich resonant voice sang, Minuit Chrétiens. The cannonade ceased and when the hymn finished applause broke out from our side and from the German trenches! The Germans were celebrating Christmas too and we could hear them singing two hundred yards from us. Now I am going to tell you something which you will think incredible but I give you my word that it is true. At dawn the Germans displayed a placard over the trenches on which was written Happy Christmas. then leaving their trenches, unarmed they advanced towards us singing and shouting "com-

rades!". No one fired. We also had left our trenches and separated from each other only by the half frozen Yes, we exchanged presents ... Was it not splendid? Think you that we were wrong? We have been criticised here; it is said that we ought to have fired. But would it not have been dastardly? And then, why kill one another on such a festive day?

a Belgian soldier

Minuit, Chrétiens

Minuit, chrétiens, c'est l'heure solennelle
Où l'Homme-Dieu descendit jusqu'à nous,
Pour effacer la tache originelle,
Et de son Père arrêter le courroux.
Le monde entier tressaille d'espérance,
À cette nuit qui lui donne un Sauveur.
Peuple, à genoux, attends ta délivrance
Noël! Noël! Voici le Rédempteur!
Noël! Noël! Voici le Rédempteur!

Midnight, Christians, it is the solemn hour
When God as man descended among us
To expunge the stain of original sin
And to put an end to the wrath of his father.
The entire world thrills with hope
On this night which gives us a savior.
People, on your knees, attend your deliverance.
Christmas! Christmas! Here is the Redeemer!
Christmas! Christmas! Here is the Redeemer!

Minuit, Chrétiens, above literally translated, is the hymn that we know as **O Holy Night** which was translated to English by John Sullivan Dwight (1813–1893)

O holy night, the stars are brightly shining,
It is the night of the dear Savior's birth;
Long lay the world in sin and error pining,
Till He appeared and the soul felt its worth.
A thrill of hope the weary world rejoices,
For yonder breaks a new and glorious morn.

The third verse is most stunning in light of the war that surrounded these men:

Le Rédempteur a brisé toute entrave,
La Terre est libre et le Ciel est ouvert.
Il voit un frère où n'était qu'un esclave,
L'amour unit ceux qu'enchaînait le fer.
Qui lui dira notre reconnaissance?
C'est pour nous tous qu'il naît, qu'il souffre et meurt.
Peuple, debout! Chante ta délivrance.
Noël! Noël! Chantons le Rédempteur!
Noël! Noël! Chantons le Rédempteur!

The Redeemer has broken all shackles.
The earth is free and heaven is open.
He sees a brother were there was once but a slave;
Love unites those who restrain the sword.
Who will tell him our gratitude?
It is for us all that he was born, that he suffered and died.
People, stand up, sing your deliverance!
Christmas! Christmas! Let us sing the Redeemer!
Christmas! Christmas! Let us sing the Redeemer!

Truly He taught us to love one another
His law is love and His gospel is peace
Chains shall He break, for the slave is our brother,
And in His name all oppression shall cease.
Sweet hymns of joy in grateful chorus raise we,
Let all within us praise His holy name.

*O*n Christmas Eve, as each fireball went up from the German lines, our men shouted 'Hurrah' and 'Let's have another'. They also sang **'Christians, Awake!'** and other Christmas hymns. On Christmas Day one of the Germans came out of the trenches and held his hands up. Our fellows immediately got out of their trenches and the Germans got out of their's, and we met in the middle, and for the rest of the day we fraternised, exchange food, cigarettes and souvenirs. The Germans gave us some of their sausages, and we gave them some of our stuff. The Scotsmen started the bagpipes, and we had a rare old jollification, which included football, in which the Germans took part. The Germans expressed themselves as being tired of the war and wished it was over. They greatly admired our equipment and wanted to exchange jack-knives and other articles. Next day we got an order that all communication and friendly intercourse with the enemy must cease, but we did not fire at all that day, and the Germans did not fire at us.

Sergeant Major Frank Naden

Christians, Awake

Christians, awake, salute the happy morn
Whereon the Saviour of the world was born
Rise to adore the mystery of love
Which hosts of angels chanted from above
With them the joyful tidings first begun
Of God incarnate and the Virgin's Son

Then to the watchful shepherds it was told
Who heard the angelic herald's voice: "Behold,
I bring good tidings of a Saviour's birth
To you and all the nations upon earth
This day hath God fulfilled His promised word;
This day is born a Saviour, Christ the Lord."

He spake, and straightaway the celestial choir
In hymns of joy, unknown before, conspire
The praises of redeeming love they sang
And heaven's whole orb with alleluias rang
God's highest glory was their anthem still
Peace upon earth and unto men goodwill

To Bethlehem straight the shepherds ran
To see the wonder God had wrought for man
And found, with Joseph and the blessed Maid
Her Son, the Saviour, in a manger laid
Amazed, the wondrous story they proclaim
The earliest heralds of the Saviour's name

Let us, like these good shepherds, them employ
Our grateful voices to proclaim the joy
Trace we the Babe, who hath retrieved our loss
From His poor manger to His bitter cross
Treading His steps, assisted by His grace
Till man's first heavenly state again takes place

Then may we hope, the angelic thrones among
To sing, redeemed, a glad triumphal song
He that was born upon this joyful day
Around us all His glory shall display
Saved by His love, incessant we shall sing
Of angels and of angel-men the King.

*T*he Scots Guards and the Germans opposite, by mutual consent, mixed freely with each other. They exchanged addresses, and promised to write to each other – a typical habit of Tommy's. Two of the German officers took dinner with our two officers, and before they left arranged to play a football match on New Year Day. Six of the Worcesters had lunch in the German lines, and the same number of Germans had lunch in ours. Before parting, it was arranged that before firing recommenced on either side three volleys should be fired in the air. A week from now these men on both sides will be doing almost unspeakable things in order to kill each other.

A dispatch rider

*I*t was rather wonderful: the night was clear, cold and frosty and across to our lines at this unusually miserable hour of need came the sound of such tunes very well played, especially by a man with a cornet who is probably well known. Christmas day was very misty and out came these Germans to wish us "a happy day"; we went out [and] told them we were at war with them and that really they must play the game and pretend to fight; they went back but again attempted to come towards us so we fired over their heads; they fired a shot back to show they understood and the rest of the day passed quietly in this part of the line, but in others a deal of fraternising went on. So there you are; all this talk of hate, all this firing at each other that has raged since the beginning of the war quelled and stayed by the magic of Christmas. Indeed one German said "But you are of the same religion as us and today is the day of peace! It is really a great triumph for the church. It is a great hope for future peace when two great nations hating each other *as foes have seldom hated, one side vowing eternal hate and vengeance and setting their venom to music, should on Christmas day and for all that the word implies, lay down their arms, exchange smokes and wish each other happiness.*

An officer

*C*hristmas Day! The most wonderful day on record. In the early hours of the morning the events of last night appeared as some weird dream – but to-day, well, it beggars description. You will hardly credit what I am going to tell you. Listen. Last night as I sat in my little dug-out, writing, my chum came bursting in upon me with: "Bob! hark at 'em!" And I listened. From the German trenches came the sound of music and singing. My chum continued. "They've got Christmas trees all along the top of their trenches I Never saw such a sight!". Climbing the parapet, I saw a sight which I shall remember to my dying day. Right along the whole of their line were hung paper lanterns and illuminations of every description, many of them in such positions as to suggest that they were hung upon Christmas trees.

Sergeant A. Lovell

*O*n Christmas Eve it froze hard, and Christmas day dawned on an appropriately sparkling landscape. The dead on both sides had been lying out in the open since the fierce night fighting of a week earlier. When I got out I found a large crowd of officers and men, English and German, grouped around the bodies, which had already been gathered together and laid out in rows. It was a ghastly sight. The digging parties were busy on the two big common graves, but the ground was hard and the work was slow and laborious. In the intervals of superintending it we chatted with the Germans, most of whom were quite affable. The digging completed, the graves were filled in, and the German officers remained to pay their tribute of respect while our chaplain read a short service. It was one of the most impressive things I have ever witnessed. Friend and foe stood side by side, bare-headed, watching tall, grave figure of the padre outlined against the frosty landscape as he blessed the poor broken bodies at his feet. Then with more formal salutes we turned and made our way back to out respective ruts.

A soldier

*H*ere we were on Christmas day, and a jolly time we had. We had a ripping dinner of real good hot stew, home plum pudding and other 'goodies'. We had a mutual understanding with the Germans not to shoot, and went out past our firing line, talking to them and exchanging greetings, chocolate, and cigarettes, and we also sang carols and hymns at their request. It was good to have peace on Christmas Day. I have had cards from the King and Queen and a present from Princess Mary; all these I shall treasure.

Corporal A. Ashford, to his father,
a Congregational minister

*W*hat a strange Christmas Eve it was! Soldiers from both sides singing to each other, songs, hymns, and carols, and walking around bonfires. We came out of the trenches later on in the evening, and went into supports. And for once, we were sorry to leave the trenches for we felt 'Christmas day' in the trenches was going to be a remarkable day, Even on Christmas Eve the firing ceased by common consent. At about two o'clock on Christmas morning a German band came out of the trenches and played carols, 'Home Sweet Home,' 'Christmas, awake,' etc. It was wonderful to hear. Some of our men who wear in the trenches on Christmas Day told us the Germans were a fine set of fellows, and many could talk good English

Lance Corporal J.S. Calder

*T*hen they started to sing, and when they finished our fellows started singing back to them, but the climax was reached on the afternoon of Christmas Day. We invited each other to come over unarmed. So a party of us got out of the trench and went over to meet a party of them at the barbed wire in the centre of the field. They all shook hands with us and no one could have greeted better than they did. They gave us presents of cigarettes and cigars and we all exchanged souvenirs. One gave me his cap for my Balaclava cap. Most of them could speak English. Their officers were over as well as ours. The German officers wanted British newspapers, and we gave them a pile of old ones. They wanted to arrange a football match with us but it got rather too late. When we parted they all shook hands and gave us a cheer. Of course we cheered in return. One of their officers told us he had lived a number of years in Glasgow. It hardly seems possible for such a thing to happen – deadly enemies to go forth and meet each other with all goodwill and then return to the trenches and shoot the first *man who showed himself. I suppose it is one of the mysteries of human nature.*

A soldier

We had the time of our lives on Christmas Day. The Germans left their trenches and walked without their rifles half-way across the field to where we were entrenched. There was not a shot fired. Some of our chaps then got out and went to meet the German soldiers. You should have seen them shaking hands with our boys and handing them smokes. Both sides walked and talked with one another as if there was nothing the matter. Later on our lads helped the Germans to bury their dead and sang over the graves. It was a sight you could never forget.

Lance Corporal George Yearsley

This will be the most memorable Christmas I've ever spent or likely to spend: since about tea time yesterday I don't think there's been a shot fired on either side up to now. Last night turned a very clear frost moonlight night, so soon after dusk we had some decent fires going and had a few carols and songs. The Germans commenced by placing lights all along the edge of their trenches and coming over to us – wishing us a Happy Christmas ... In spite of our fires etc. it was terribly cold and a job to sleep between look out duties, which are two hours in every six. First thing this morning it was very foggy. So we stood to arms a little longer than usual. A few of us that were lucky could go to Holy Communion early this morning. It was celebrated in a ruined farm about 500 yds behind us. I unfortunately couldn't go. There must be something in the spirit of Christmas as to day we are all on top of our trenches running about. Whereas other days we have to keep our heads well down. ...

*About 10$\underline{^{30}}$ we had a short church parade, the morning service etc. held in the trench. How we did sing. – **O come all ye faithful**. And **While shepherds watched their flocks by night** were the hymns we had. At present we are cooking our Christmas Dinner! so will finish this letter later. Dinner is over! and well we enjoyed it. Our dinner party started off with fried bacon and dip-bread: followed by hot Xmas Pudding. I had a mascot in my piece. Next item on the menu was muscatels and almonds, oranges, bananas, chocolate etc followed by cocoa and smokes. You can guess we thought of the dinners at home. Just before dinner I had the pleasure of shaking hands with several Germans: a party of them came 1/2way over to us so several of us went out to them. I exchanged one of my balaclavas for a hat. I've also got a button off one of their tunics. We also exchanged smokes etc. and had a decent chat. They say they won't fire tomorrow if we don't so I suppose we shall get a bit of a holiday – perhaps. After exchanging autographs and them wishing us a Happy New Year we departed and came back and had our dinner. We can hardly believe that we've been firing at them for the last week or two – it all seems so strange. At present its freezing hard and everything is covered with ice ...".*

... As I can't explain to everyone how I spent my 25th – you might hand this round please,

There are plenty of huge shell holes in front of our trenches, also pieces of shrapnel to be found. I never expected to shake hands with Germans between the firing lines on Christmas Day and I don't suppose you thought of us doing so. So after a fashion we've en-

joyed? our Christmas. Hoping you spend a happy time also George Boy as well. How we thought of England during the day.

Kind regards to all the neighbours.
With much love from Boy

Oh Come, All Ye Faithful

O come, all ye faithful,
Joyful and triumphant,
O come ye, O come ye to Bethlehem;
Come and behold him,
Born the King of angels;
O come, let us adore him,
O come, let us adore him,
O Come, let us adore him, Christ the Lord.

God of God,
Light of Light,
Lo! he abhors not the Virgin's womb:
Very God,
Begotten, not created; Refrain

Sing, choirs of angels,
Sing in exultation,
Sing, all ye citizens of heaven above;
Glory to God
In the highest; Refrain

See how the shepherds,
Summoned to his cradle,
Leaving their flocks, draw nigh to gaze;
We too will thither
Bend our joyful footsteps.

While Shepherds Watched Their Flocks

While Shepherds watch their flocks by night
All seated on the ground
The angel of the Lord came down
And glory shone around
"Fear not," said he for mighty dread
had seized their troubled mind
"Glad tidings of great joy I bring
To you and all man-kind"

"To you in David's town this day
Is born of David's line
The Savior who is Christ the Lord
And this shall me the sign
The heavenly babe you there shall find
To human view displayed
All meanly wrapped in swathing bands
And in a manger laid"

Those spoke the seraph and forth-with
Appeared a shing throng
Of angels praising God who thus
Addressed their joyful song
"All glory be to God on high
And on the earth be peace
Goodwill hence-forth from heaven to men
Begin and never cease"

Christmas Wanes: Ending the Truces

For those soldiers abiding in the fields of Flanders, the earthly peace of that Christmas varied in length, in some places lasting only the few hours of that Holy Day. In other places along the trenches it lasted for days or even weeks. Those truces did end but God's eternal peace had made its mark on many souls.

In 1914, all attempts to prevent any Christmas truce had failed.

Pope Benedict XV had proposed to the warring parties that they should "cease the clang of arms while Christendom celebrates the Feast of the World's Redemption."

Germany provisionally accepted that proposal but the rejection by the other 'Christian' countries ensured the death of this peace initiative. The kingdoms of this world had other ideas.

From British Corps Headquarters, an order from General Sir Horace Smith-Dorrien read:

... Experiences of this and every other war proves undoubtedly that troops in trenches, in close proximity to the enemy, slide very easily, if permitted to do so, into a 'live and let live' theory of life ... the Corp Commander therefore directs Divisional commanders to impress on subordinate commanders the absolute necessity of encouraging an offensive spirit ... unofficial armistices, however tempting and amusing they be, are absolutely prohibited.

[One description of the soldiers' situation in the Great War was that it was a war in which lions were led by donkeys.]

In Germany, on hearing the news of the Christmas truce, an editor wrote, "we say with sorrow regarding the makers and participants of these overtures that they have a clouded understanding of this situation's gravity."

Like that newspaper editor who was far away from the bloodbath and safe in his dry and warm home, the Army brass were also perturbed. They published an order which proscribed any such future events: "All acts contrary to this order will be punished as high treason."

But the true treason of that season was against the Kingdom of God in their midst. How easily the din created by the arrogance of power drowns out the words of the Christ born at Bethlehem.

How quickly Christians are swayed by their earthly kings to forget the words of their Commander.

"By this shall all men know that ye are my disciples, if ye have love one to another."

Jesus

One Christian of that generation briefly wrote of his romantic view of the Great War. In 1914, he was not in the trenches but in studies. But in 1917, at Oxford, he received his commission and was sent to the front. During his sixth month there, he was wounded. April, 1918, brought to an end his brief stint on that battlefield.

Over two decades later, after he had became a Christian, he imagined the scenario of drawing a bead on a German soldier who was at the same moment aiming a rifle at him. As eternity claimed them both, they embraced in Heaven.

Of course, the real possibility of that outcome has no bearing on this question: Is a Christian obeying his heavenly King's voice when he seeks to kill his brother?

Providentially, C.S. Lewis lived through that Great War and the world is much the richer.

"'Love your neighbor as yourself.' Love does no harm to its neighbor."

Paul

And he [Jesus] opened his mouth, and taught them, saying,

Blessed are the poor in spirit: for theirs is the kingdom of heaven.

Blessed are they that mourn: for they shall be comforted.

Blessed are the meek: for they shall inherit the earth.

Blessed are they which do hunger and thirst after righteousness: for they shall be filled.

Blessed are the merciful: for they shall obtain mercy.

Blessed are the pure in heart: for they shall see God.

Blessed are the peacemakers: for they shall be called the children of God.

Blessed are they which are persecuted for righteousness' sake: for theirs is the kingdom of heaven.

Blessed are ye, when men shall revile you, and persecute you, and shall say all manner of evil against you falsely, for my sake.

Rejoice, and be exceeding glad: for great is your reward in heaven: for so persecuted they the prophets which were before you.

The Cousins:
Tragedy and Triumph

Tragedy marked the Great War from its beginnings.

In Sarajevo, on 28 June, 1914, Archduke Franz Ferdinand, heir to the Austro-Hungarian throne, and his wife, Sophie, were murdered. She had joined him on his official visit there. 28 June marked the anniversary of Franz Ferdinand's signing the agreement that had allowed their wedding of 1 July. [He had had to renounce any claims to the throne for his future children as Sophie was not of the correct 'upper crust.'] Ferdinand's dying words were, "Sophie dear! Sophie dear! Don't Die! Stay alive for our children!" She was expecting their fourth child.

The first attempt on the Archduke's life had failed. A grenade hurled at his car had missed, but those in the car behind him had been wounded. Later, the Archduke and his wife decided to go to the hospital to see the two seriously injured men. Enroute, the driver made a wrong turn. He stopped and backed up. The name of the street was Franz Joseph.

Standing nearby, believing that they had failed in their mission, was one of the revolutionaries, a nineteen-year-old failed student who had been rejected from military service. He advanced toward the car and shot them.

Decades later, the spot was marked with this hope, "May Peace Prevail on Earth."

Peace did not prevail then.

Heir to the throne, Franz Ferdinand had been shot. His voice of restraint was now silent.
In the days ahead, the hawks took unfettered flight. Vienna was hell-bent on having a war. As Kaiser Wilhelm noted, Vienna's ultimatum to Serbia on 23 July was deliberately worded so as to ensure its failure. Vienna declared war on 28 July.

Now, the urgent task of averting a wider war fell into the hands of Germany and Russia. German Kaiser Wilhelm II and Russian Czar Nicholas II were cousins. They, along with Britain's King George V, all sprang from the linage of Queen Victoria, their grandmother.

These letters between them display their affection for each other and their failure to avert war. They address each other by their childhood nicknames, Willy and Nicky.

Berlin 3/I/13

Dearest Nicky

*T*he messenger leaves today with my presents for you Alix and the children. I hope that they may please the august recipients. At the same time I send you my heartiest wishes for Xmas and a peaceful New Year. I earnestly hope and trust that 1913 may prove a peaceful one, as you telegraphed to me on New Years day. I think that on the whole the outlook is reassuring ...

Up to now we have had a warm snowless winter here, which allows us to indulge in nice long gallops on horseback, nearly every day, provided it does not pour with rain.

Goodbye dearest Nicky, my best love to Alix and the children especially to the boy, who I hope is getting better, and believe myself Ever

Your most aff-ate cousin and friend

Willy

Berlin 3/II/13

Dearest Nicky

*S*o many thanks for your kind wishes and the splendid gift you so kindly sent me. What a great surprise when I entered my birthday room and saw the two grand pictures. It was really a charming idea of yours to send me those two beautiful originals which are of great artistical and historical value to us here, as they represent portraits of so many well known personality here. These pictures gave me a real great pleasure, and I beg you to accept my most hearty thanks once more.

I am so glad to see by your letter, that the dear boy is making good progress, but sorry that the state of Alix's health is not satisfactory, I am sure the weeks she spent in tending the boy, must have been most trying; but confidently hope that rest and a cure or the Crimea will soon put her to right again.

I fervently hope with you that the Balkan troubles may soon be finally arranged without further complications, and am most anxious to cooperate with you for that purpose. Of course Austria as a near neighbour to those parts has interests to look after. But I am under the impression that in doing so, she does not reclaim anything for herself, but only wishes to make sure that no readjustments of the map occur which might turn out a danger to her in future. Adalbert is again out of bed, and tomorrow Dona will again take up her quarters together with me. Thank God all went off so well. Best love to Alix and the children and believe me

Ever
Your most devoted and aff-ate cousin

Willy

Berlin 18/III/1913

Dearest Nicky

Mᵃy I inform you that we have now definitely fixed the date for the wedding of our dear Sissy for the 24ᵗʰ of May.

The main object of my lines is to convey to you and Alix our most cordial invitation to the wedding ceremonies. We both would only be too delighted if you could give us the pleasure of your presence and I fervently hope that you will be able to leave Russia for a few days to meet many of your relatives; as we have asked your dear Mama, Aunt Alix, Georgie and May, Waldemar etc. to enable all the "Geschwister" to meet each other as well as Aunt Thyra.

I am so glad all your festivities went off so well and successfully, and that your boy could be present, and that he is progressing satisfactorily, and will soon I hope have quite recovered. After Easter the Cumberlands are coming for a visit and then we go to Hamburg for a month, as the damned Balkan muddle has deprived me of the possibility of beeing at my heavenly paradise Corfu!

With best love from Victoria and me to Alix and all the children believe me Ever your most devoted cousin and friend

Willy

Dearest Nicky

*M*any thanks to you dear Alix and the children *for your kind wishes and the lovely china pot which accompanied them. Thank God I could spend my birthday in happiness especially owing to the presence of dear Sophy and Georgy who had come all the way from Athen to spend the day with me. I am most gratified that you still keep pleasant recollections of the visit you paid us last summer on the occasion of Sissy's wedding, and you may be assured that we all most heartily reciprocate your kind feelings and re-membrance.*

I am so glad to hear that you all have benefited so much by your nice stay in the Crimea, and that especially Alix and the boy are so much better for their visit to the sunny South.

Remember the interest, which you took a few years ago, when you visited Homburg, and saw the cathedral I built there, I venture to present you with a book, which I have caused to be published about the Chapel in the New Castle of Posen.

It is in the old Byzantine Style, took 7 years work and was consecreted in our presence last August. It is copied from Motives partly from Ravenna (Theodoric the Great's tomb) partly from Mon Reale and the Capella Palatina in Palermo.

The mission of Bieloselsky who brought the cravat for Alix's Dragoons was a very kind thought and most appreciated by the Regiment; he is to lunch with me on

Sunday. With best love to Alix and the dear children believe me, dearest Nicky

Ever your devoted cousin and friend

Willy

The following flurry of telegrams sought to avert a wider war after Vienna declared war on Serbia.

The Willy-Nicky Telegrams

The Kaiser's letters to the Tsar, copied from the government archives in Petrograd, and brought from Russia by Isaac Don Levine, ed., intro. by N.F. Grant. London, Hodder and Stoughton Ltd, 1920.

From Czar Nicholas to Kaiser Wilhelm:
Peter's Court Palais, 29 July 1914

Sa Majesté l'Empereur, Neues Palais

*A*m glad you are back. In this serious moment, I appeal to you to help me. An ignoble war has been declared to a weak country. The indignation in Russia shared fully by me is enormous. I foresee that very soon I shall be overwhelmed by the pressure forced upon me and be forced to take extreme measures which will lead to war. To try and avoid such a calamity as a European war I beg you in the name of our old friendship to do what you can to stop your allies from going too far.

Nicky

From Kaiser Wilhelm to Czar Nicholas:

28 July 1914

It is with the gravest concern that I hear of the impression which the action of Austria against Serbia is creating in your country. The unscrupulous agitation that has been going on in Serbia for years has resulted in the outrageous crime, to which Archduke Francis Ferdinand fell a victim. The spirit that led Serbians to murder their own king and his wife still dominates the country. You will doubtless agree with me that we both, you and me, have a common interest as well as all Sovereigns to insist that all the persons morally responsible for the dastardly murder should receive their deserved punishment. In this case politics plays no part at all.

On the other hand, I fully understand how difficult it is for you and your Government to face the drift of your public opinion. Therefore, with regard to the hearty and tender friendship which binds us both from long ago with firm ties, I am exerting my utmost influence to induce the Austrians to deal straightly to arrive to a satisfactory understanding with you. I confidently hope that you will help me in my efforts to smooth over difficulties that may still arise.

Your very sincere and devoted friend and cousin

Willy

From Kaiser Wilhelm to Czar Nicholas:

Berlin, 29 July 1914

I received your telegram and share your wish that peace should be maintained. But as I told you in my first telegram, I cannot consider Austria's action against Servia an "ignoble" war. Austria knows by experience that Servian promises on paper are wholly unreliable. I understand its action must be judged as trending to get full guarantee that the Servian promises shall become real facts. This my reasoning is borne out by the statement of the Austrian cabinet that Austria does not want to make any territorial conquests at the expense of Servia. I therefore suggest that it would be quite possible for Russia to remain a spectator of the austro-servian conflict without involving Europe in the most horrible war she ever witnessed. I think a direct understanding between your Government and Vienna possible and desirable, and as I already telegraphed to you, my Government is continuing its exercises to promote it. Of course military measures on the part of Russia would be looked upon by Austria as a calamity we both wish to avoid and jeopardize my position as mediator which I readily accepted on your appeal to my friendship and my help.

Willy

From Czar Nicholas to Kaiser Wilhelm:

Peter's Court Palace, 29 July 1914

T hanks for your telegram conciliatory and friendly. Whereas official message presented today by your ambassador to my minister was conveyed *in a very different tone. Beg you to explain this divergency! It would be right to give over the Austro-servian problem to the Hague conference. Trust in your wisdom and friendship.*

Your loving Nicky

From Czar Nicholas to Kaiser Wilhelm:

Peter's Court Palais, 30 July 1914

*T*hank you heartily for your quick answer. Am sending Tatischev this evening with instructions. The military measures which have now come into force were decided five days ago for reasons of defence on account of Austria's preparations. I hope from all my heart that these measures won't in any way interfere with your part as mediator which I greatly value. We need your strong pressure on Austria to come to an understanding with us.*

Nicky

From Kaiser Wilhelm to Czar Nicholas:

[Sent at 1:20 A.M.]

Berlin, 30 July 1914

*B*est thanks for telegram. It is quite out of the question that my ambassadors language could have been in contradiction with the tenor of my telegram. Count Pourtalès was instructed to draw the attention of your government to the danger & grave consequences involved by a mobilisation; I said the*

*same in my telegram to you. Austria has only mobil-
ised against Servia & only a part of her army. If, as
it is now the case, according to the communication by
you & your Government, Russia mobilises against
Austria, my rôle as mediator you kindly intrusted me
with, & which I accepted at you[r] express prayer, will
be endangered if not ruined. The whole weight of the
decision lies solely on you[r] shoulders now, who have
to bear the responsibility for Peace or War.*

Willy

From Kaiser Wilhelm to Czar Nicholas:

Berlin, 31 July 1914

*O*n your appeal to my friendship and your call
*for assistance began to mediate between your
and the austro-hungarian Government. While
this action was proceeding your troops were mobilised
against Austro-Hungary, my ally. thereby, as I have
already pointed out to you, my mediation has been
made almost illusory.*

*I have nevertheless continued my action. I now re-
ceive authentic news of serious preparations for war
on my Eastern frontier. Responsibility for the safety
of my empire forces preventive measures of defence
upon me. In my endeavours to maintain the peace of
the world I have gone to the utmost limit possible. The
responsibility for the disaster which is now threatening the whole civilized world will not be laid at my
door. In this moment it still lies in your power to avert
it. Nobody is threatening the honour or power of Russia who can well afford to await the result of my mediation. My friendship for you and your empire, trans-*

mitted to me by my grandfather on his deathbed has always been sacred to me and I have honestly often backed up Russia when she was in serious trouble especially in her last war.

The peace of Europe may still be maintained by you, if Russia will agree to stop the milit. measures which must threaten Germany and Austro-Hungary.

Willy

From Czar Nicholas to Kaiser Wilhelm:
['Crossed in the mail' with the previous telegram]

Sa Majesté l'Empereur, Neues Palais

I thank you heartily for your mediation which begins to give one hope that all may yet end peacefully. It is technically impossible to stop our military preparations which were obligatory owing to Austria's mobilisation. We are far from wishing war. As long as the negociations with Austria on Servia's account are taking place my troops shall not make any provocative action. I give you my solemn word for this. I put all my trust in Gods mercy and hope in your successful mediation in Vienna for the welfare of our countries and for the peace of Europe.

Your affectionate

Nicky

From Czar Nicholas to Kaiser Wilhelm:

Peter's Court, Palace, 1 August 1914

Sa Majesté l'Empereur, Berlin

I received your telegram. Understand you are obliged to mobilise but wish to have the same guarantee from you as I gave you, that these measures do not mean war and that we shall continue negociating for the benefit of our countries and universal peace deal to all our hearts. Our long proved friendship must succeed, with God's help, in avoiding bloodshed. Anexiously, full of confidence await your answer.

Nicky

From Kaiser Wilhelm to Czar Nicholas:

Berlin, 1 August 1914

Thanks for your telegram. I yesterday pointed out to your government the way by which alone war may be avoided. Although I requested an answer for noon today, no telegram from my ambassador conveying an answer from your Government has reached me as yet. I therefore have been obliged to mobilise my army.

Immediate affirmative clear and unmistakable answer from your government is the only way to avoid endless misery. Until I have received this answer alas, I am unable to discuss the subject of your telegram. As a matter of fact I must request you to immediately or-

der your troops on no account to commit the slightest
act of trespassing over our frontiers.

Willy

The sad fact is that this same day, Germany declared
war on Russia. While the event of the birth of Christ
would bring peace to the battlefield in December,
now, it gained no foothold in the attempts to avert
world war.

On 3 August, Germany declared war on France. On 4
August, Britain declared war on Germany.

King George encouraged his troops as they left with
this:

**My message to the troops of the Expeditionary
Force.**

Aug. 12th 1914.

*You are leaving home to fight for the safety and
honour of my Empire. Belgium, whose country
we are pledged to defend, has been attacked
and France is about to be invaded by the same pow-
erful foe. I have implicit confidence in you my soldiers.
Duty is your watchword, and I know your duty will be
nobly done.*

*I shall follow your every movement with deepest inter-
est and mark with eager satisfaction your daily progress, indeed your welfare will never be absent from
my thoughts.*

I pray God to bless you and guard you and bring you back victorious.

All these warring parties sought to save their empires. All of them lost them. The Great War was their death knell. The end came for the Austro-Hungarian Empire, the Ottoman Empire, the Russian Empire, and the German Empire. And the stage had been set for the long spiral downward of the once imperial British Empire.

In passing, it is interesting to note that the titles taken for the rulers of Germany and Russia, Kaiser and Czar, were derived from the title Caesar, whose empire also passed away.

Men's barbarous actions while seeking to preserve their kingdoms brings to mind the words of the King of another Kingdom, the one whose birth was celebrated by enemies and brothers that Christmas Day in 1914, "Whosoever shall seek to save his life shall lose it; and whosoever shall lose his life shall preserve it."

Following that first 'Christmas' so long ago, two other cousins stepped onto the world stage. The first was John the Baptist of whom it was said at his birth, several months before the birth of Jesus,

And thou, child, shalt be called the prophet of the Highest: for thou shalt go before the face of the Lord to prepare his ways;

To give knowledge of salvation unto his people by the remission of their sins,

Through the tender mercy of our God; whereby the dayspring from on high hath visited us,

To give light to them that sit in darkness and in the shadow of death, to guide our feet into the way of peace ...

Before the births of both John and Jesus, Mary had been told,

Fear not, Mary: for thou hast found favour with God.

And, behold, thou shalt conceive in thy womb, and bring forth a son, and shalt call his name JE-SUS.

He shall be great, and shall be called the Son of the Highest: and the Lord God shall give unto him the throne of his father David:

And he shall reign over the house of Jacob for ever; and of his kingdom there shall be no end.

And His kingdom is still with us.

Neither Jesus nor John sought to save his life or his position.

John told his disciples that his ministry must decrease and that of Christ must increase. In the end, he was beheaded because he spoke the truth, which was not what the adulterous wife of his earthly king wanted to hear.

Jesus spoke the truth "as no other man." For that, he was nailed to a cross. He gave up his life that we might have eternal life through him, in a Kingdom that shall never end.

Armistice: The Ending of Hostilities

In December of 1917, the armistice between Germany and Russia ended the battle on the Eastern Front. But it would be another Christmas and almost another year before the Great War would reach its conclusion.

Along the Western Front, on that Christmas Eve, one young Marine wrote home that "it's a dismal thing, I bet, to spend Christmas in the trenches and it seems a sacrilege that the terrible master that has ridden Europe for the past 3 years will soon have another new one to desecrate with his guns ..."

As American military men had just entered the war that summer, in all probability they had never heard about the truce at Christmas in 1914 – a truce that was never repeated in as wide a scope. In 1915, however, a German soldier described one similar event: "When the Christmas bells sounded in the villages of the Vosges behind the lines ... something fantastically unmilitary occurred. German and French troops spontaneously made peace and ceased hostilities; they visited each other through disused trench tunnels, and exchanged wine, cognac and cigarettes for Westphalian black bread, biscuits and ham. This suited them so well that they remained good friends even after Christmas was over." [In 1919, this soldier, Richard Schirrmann, founded the first Youth Hostel Association.]

After 1914, the war had become even more brutal. Poisonous gas entered the scene of warfare. Chlorine, phosgene, and mustard gas brought more deaths and suffering. And flamethrowers introduced their own distinctive terror and death. The introduction of tanks brought a third new terror, but undoubtedly, they saved many lives from the savage machine gun fire.

And then there were many more bloody battles like Belleau Wood, in June of 1918, after which, the Fifth Marines would forever wear the French Fourragere. The name of the wood was changed from Bois de Belleau to Bois de la Brigade de Marine. The appellation, Devil Dogs, given to the Marines, epitomized the fierceness of the combat, which persisted right up to the very hour that the armistice would take effect.

By October of 1918, everywhere, hopes were rising for an armistice. In the first week, Austria-Hungary and Germany had sent notes to the United States, seeking an armistice based on President Woodrow Wilson's "Fourteen Points."

On 11 November, the warring parties signed the armistice, bringing that great bloodbath to an end. Only those who suffered through those cataclysmic events truly understood the meaning of that day.

On the Continent, Russia and Germany had each seen 1.7 million of their own soldiers slaughtered. Between them, some 9 million were wounded.

France saw 1.3 million of its soldiers sacrificed, and over 4 million wounded. Austria-Hungary suffered about the same number of tragic loses.

Great Britain mourned almost a million soldiers and twice that number suffered wounds.

The United States, which had only been in the war for a year and some months (but a very long year for those military men), saw over 100,000 of its own men killed and over a quarter million wounded.

The deep meaning of that armistice remained in the minds of World War I veterans a half century later when the U.S. Congress, in one of its clueless moves, changed the observance of the federal holiday from November 11th to a certain Monday of October. Memorial Day, Veterans Day and Washington's Birthday were all moved on the calendar in order to create three-day federal holiday weekends.

Because of the war that had followed that "War to End All Wars," President Eisenhower had signed a law that broadened the meaning of "Armistice Day" by making it "Veterans Day" in 1954. But in the minds of the World War I generation, the memory of that armistice still held sway.

So, in the late 1960s when Congress changed the date, I can still remember my grandmother adamantly asserting that Armistice Day was November 11th, NOT the fourth Monday of October. The thousands of soldiers who, like my grandfather, had served in France and other lands would not hear of such a change.

So, South Dakota and Mississippi refused to follow the federal lead. And one by one, the other states began reverting back to the November 11th observance. And the politicians received an earful. The World War I generation was still alive and well; remembering and speaking up. They again took back lost ground.

The end result was that one decade after changing the date, Congress, in 1978, restored the observance to November 11th.

The height and depth of the longing for an end to that bloody war was revealed in the celebrations that broke out on November 7, 1918. Following a reply to the German government from President Wilson, on that date, the Chief of Staff of the German Army, von Hindenburg, sent a telegram to the Allied Supreme Commander seeking a date for negotiating that armistice. A mistaken news report declared that the armistice had been signed. And despite all attempts by capitols and headquarters to correct the mistake, celebrations broke out around the world.

Newspaper "Extras" proclaimed "Peace." Workers and students poured into the streets with whistles and bells and anything that could make noise. Church bells pealed. Parades processed. Jubilation went unquenched. And it started all over again, four days later, on the 11th of November.

In one dishonorable aspect, the rejoicing on the home front differed markedly from that on the battlefield. All across the U.S., effigies of 'Kaiser Bill' were hung or burned. In Kansas, a Mennonite farmer was kidnapped and beaten. The work of the propagandists bore ugly fruit.

But in the trenches, there were scenes resembling that setting of almost four years earlier on Christmas Day, 1914. Shaking hands, the soldiers exchanged souvenirs. Food was given to their enemies. Songs and cheers replaced gunfire.

Before those armistice rumors came to fruition, one American in battle had expressed the hope that "I shall have done with all these nightmares-waking realizations of Hell ..."

When his decimated battalion received notice of the cease-fire in the literal last minutes of the war, "The poor boys, some of them, just dropped and cried."

Now, one German soldier sighed, "Thank the good God that the war is finished."

"It is finished" marked another epoch, the one begun with the birth of that babe at Bethlehem. There, shepherds had heard of "peace, good will toward men" – peace because, in Jesus "was life, and the life was the light of men;" peace because Jesus' sacrificial death on the cross paid the debt for our sin; peace because "as many as received him, to them gave he power to become the children of God, even to them that believe on his name" (John 1).

Now, we give thanks to God that "it is finished." We celebrate the birth of Jesus which led to his resurrection – His victory; our victory.

There on the battlefield, celebrations broke out. In one French village the Padre held a thanksgiving service. In Belgium, a Canadian officer, prayerbook in hand, led the thanksgiving. Then they played football.

Soldiers' eyes were now fixed on their return home. Typical are these letters:

Somewhere in France.
Nov. 27, 1918.

Dear Friends and Folks at Ruthven:

*W*ill this morning try and write you all a few lines, letting you all know I am well and that I came out of the scrap unhurt. I certainly consider myself a very lucky doughboy ... It was on the *morning of the 11*th *when we were ordered to halt. The armistice had been signed and would be over at 11 o'clock that very morning. The big guns were still roaring from both sides. We waited. Course we had all our watches out, and when 11 o'clock came sure enough it all became quiet. It almost felt like we could hear a needle drop. Then all at once came loud shrills of whistles from everywhere all along the lines with shouts of joy, the war is over. It didn't seem real to us. We sure were some happy Yanks. Wasn't long before the talk all over the line was of home. How we wished that we could just tell our folks that we were well, and that we could tell them that we would soon be on our way home ...*

With best of wishes to all my Ruthven friends. Wishing you all a Merry Christmas with ringing in a Happy New Year of Peace.

PVT. LAWRENCE M. ANDERSON,
Co. K, 358 Inf.,
American Ex. Forces

St. Sulpice, France, Dec. 19, 1918

Dear Folks,

*H*ow's everyone? I am still O.K. I have moved to another camp ... I don't know anything about coming back, but expect to be there within six *months. I hope it will be sooner.*

I hope you folks will all enjoy your Christmas. I am going to celebrate the best I can.

How are the folks near Spencer? Remember me to all of them.

What's the news back home? Have you heard anything about the rest of the boys that are in the army? ...

Unlike so many of their friends, they had made it through alive and would embrace their families again.

One soldier who was sent to the Western Front at the end of 1916 where he remained until being gassed in 1918, described the essential character of the men who had been soldiers, of those who returned home and of those who did not. After the war, in his novel, *Death of a Hero*, Richard Aldington wrote:

> *Winterbourne hated the war as much as ever, hated all the blather about it, profoundly distrusted the motives of the War partisans, and hated the Army. But he liked the soldiers, the War soldiers, not as soldiers but as men. He respected them. He was with them. With them, because they were men with fine qualities, because they had endured great hardships and dangers with simplicity, because they had parried those hardships and dangers not by hating the men who were supposed to be their enemies, but by developing a comradeship among themselves. They had every excuse for turning into brutes, and they hadn't done it. True, they were degenerating in certain ways, they were getting coarse and rough and a bit animal, but with amazing simplicity and unpretentiousness they had retained and developed a certain essential humanity and manhood. With them, then, to the end, because of their manhood*

and humanity. With them, too, because their man-
hood and humanity existed in spite of the War
and not because of it. They had saved something
from a gigantic wreck, and what they had saved
was immensely important – manhood and com-
radeship, their essential integrity as men, their
essential brotherhood as men.

It is not surprising, therefore, that in the midst of the relief and thanksgiving, there were some who were already feeling nostalgia for the soldier's life. Probably, Americans were more prone to it as they had not lived in the trenches for four long terrible years.

One American company officer voiced his feeling: "The physical relief, the absence of apprehension, brimmed us with ease and thanksgiving, but for each of us our bliss and our serenity were only the super-structure over a hidden tide of desolation and despair. Each of us was repeating to himself in his own words something I heard crying out in me: It's over, the only great thing you were ever a part of. It's over, the only heroic thing we all did together. What can you do now? ..."

The words of the Christ of Christmas come to mind, "If any man will come after me, let him deny himself, and take up his cross daily, and follow me."

In that First Century, the heroic band of his disciples changed the world forever while enduring pain and suffering and hardships. Their brothers, too, were killed. But the Kingdom for which they gave their lives is still in our midst.

Heroic bands of disciples have done great things in every century since, as they dedicated their lives to this King and His Kingdom.

The End of the Beginning

O n November 7, 1918 [the day of the pre-mature news], Orville Wright wrote from Dayton:

> We all rejoiced today to learn of the armistice just signed in Germany, which, no doubt, means the war is entirely at an end. The aeroplane has made war so terrible that I do not believe any country will again care to start a war; but I hope the allies will make another war absolutely impossible as a part of the peace terms.

What the Allies did do with their harsh 'peace' terms was to set a course which would practically ensure that this was just the end of the beginning.

In a torn land, as the smoke and darkness of the war ebbed, the light of Christ did not break through as it had on Christmas Day, 1914. Had someone put those soldiers in charge of the Armistice who, on that Christmas, embraced their enemies and gave them gifts, the chances of another great war would have been diminished.

During the war, the British Naval Blockade of Germany stopped not only military supplies, but food as well. At least three quarters of a million people in Germany died of starvation or from the effects of disease on those who were malnourished.

After the war, a report by a French lieutenant described the effects of the blockade: "Leather was appallingly short and out of 1,600 boot factories, 1,100 shut down. Children can dispense with boots but not with food. Milk, butter, and fat were very scarce. The death rate in Krupps rose from 4.1 per 1,000 in 1914 to 8.7 in 1917. The end came with a general collapse."

And despite this critical scene, Clause Twenty-six of the Armistice stated, "The existing blockade conditions ... are to remain unchanged."

The caveat given was that, supposedly, "The Allies and the United States should give consideration to the provisioning of Germany during the armistice to the extent recognized as necessary."

Germany also lost most of its commercial ships. Britain wanted no commercial competition.

The link between war and famine is shocking. In the Great War and the Russian civil war, up to 10 million people died of starvation or disease resulting from malnutrition. In Russia, peasants resorted to cannibalism. Aleksandr Solzhenitsyn wrote, "It was the result of productivity having been reduced to zero (the working hands were all carrying guns)."

The critical nature of the food shortage was emphasized in war posters in the U.S. published by the U.S. Food Administration. Poster slogans included:

Save food for world relief.

Little Americans do your bit. Eat Oatmeal ... Save the wheat for our soldiers

Cardinal Mercer has appealed ... for more food for starving millions.

Don't Waste Food while others starve!

Wheat is needed for the allies. Waste nothing.

It is our job – yours and ours – to save food so that the millions of starving people in Europe may have SOMETHING to eat.

Eat Less, Waste Nothing.

When the treaty of Versailles was signed in June of 1919, the reparations that were demanded were so harsh as to practically guarantee that the government of Germany would not be able to function or survive in the years ahead. In such chaotic circumstances, desperate and disheartened people look for a savior, but often in the wrong place.

Hew Strachan, Professor of the History of War, at Oxford University, All Souls College, wrote, "One reason why Adolf Hitler could appeal to the German people in 1933 was precisely because many genuinely convinced themselves that they had been wronged in 1919."

The dedication of Strachan's book, *The First World War*, reads, "To Pamela and Margo, who may not have lived through the First World War but have had to live with it." We all have.

The Great War was actually continued in the sequel, The Great War, Part Two. Part One had laid the groundwork that would make the Twentieth Century the bloodiest in history.

William F. Buckley, Jr., wrote that the first world war was an unnecessary war. It was also a tragic war. Part of that tragedy is seen in the failure of the cousins, the tender friends, the Kaiser and the Czar, to avert what they foresaw as a "calamity ... the most horrible war ... a disaster."

Part of the tragedy flowed from the spirit of those times. G.K. Chesterton described the character of many of the movers and shakers of his day: "They still live in the shadow of faith and have lost the light of faith."

And another piece of that tragedy which flowed from the Zeitgeist was described during the decade before the Great War by Mark Twain:

The War Prayer

It was a time of great and exalting excitement. The country was up in arms, the war was on, in every breast burned the holy fire of patriotism; the drums were beating, the bands playing, the toy pistols popping, the bunched firecrackers hissing and spluttering; on every hand and far down the receding and fading spread of roofs and balconies a fluttering wilderness of flags flashed in the sun; daily the young volunteers marched down the wide avenue gay and fine in their new uniforms, the proud fathers and mothers and sisters and sweethearts cheering them with voices choked with happy emotion as they swung by; nightly the packed mass meetings listened, panting, to patriot oratory which stirred the deepest deeps of their hearts, and which they interrupted at briefest intervals with cyclones of applause, the tears running down their cheeks the while; in the churches the pastors preached devotion to flag and country, and invoked the God of Battles beseeching His aid in our good cause in outpourings of fervid eloquence which moved every listener. It was indeed a glad and gracious time, and the half dozen rash spirits that ventured to disapprove of the war and cast a doubt upon its righteousness straightway got such a stern and angry warning that for their personal safety's sake they quickly shrank out of sight and offended no more in that way.

Sunday morning came – next day the battalions would leave for the front; the church was filled; the volunteers were there, their young faces alight with martial dreams – visions of the stern advance, the gathering momentum, the rushing charge, the flashing sabers, the flight of the foe, the tumult, the enveloping smoke, the fierce pursuit, the surrender! Then home from the war, bronzed heroes, welcomed, adored, submerged in golden seas of glory! With the volunteers sat their dear ones, proud, happy, and envied by the neighbors and friends who had no sons and brothers to send forth to the field of honor, there to win for the flag, or, failing, die the noblest of noble deaths. The service proceeded; a war chapter from the Old Testament was read; the first prayer was said; it was followed by an organ burst that shook the building, and with one impulse the house rose, with glowing eyes and beating hearts, and poured out that tremendous invocation

God the all-terrible! Thou who ordainest! Thunder thy clarion and lightning thy sword!

Then came the "long" prayer. None could remember the like of it for passionate pleading and moving and beautiful language. The burden of its supplication was, that an ever-merciful and benignant Father of us all would watch over our noble young soldiers, and aid, comfort, and encourage them in their patriotic work; bless them, shield them in the day of battle and the hour of peril, bear them in His mighty hand, make them strong and confident, invincible in the bloody onset; help them to crush the foe, grant to them and to their flag and country imperishable honor and glory.

An aged stranger entered and moved with slow and noiseless step up the main aisle, his eyes fixed upon the minister, his long body clothed in a robe that reached to his feet, his head bare, his white hair descending in a frothy cataract to his shoulders, his seamy face unnaturally pale, pale even to ghastliness. With all eyes following him and wondering, he made his silent way; without pausing, he ascended to the preacher's side and stood there waiting. With shut lids the preacher, unconscious of his presence, continued with his moving prayer, and at last finished it with the words, uttered in fervent appeal, "Bless our arms, grant us the victory, O Lord our God, Father and Protector of our land and flag!"

The stranger touched his arm, motioned him to step aside – which the startled minister did – and took his place. During some moments he surveyed the spellbound audience with solemn eyes, in which burned an uncanny light; then in a deep voice he said:

"I come from the Throne – bearing a message from Almighty God!" The words smote the house with a shock; if the stranger perceived it he gave no attention. "He has heard the prayer of His servant your shepherd, and will grant it if such shall be your desire after I, His messenger, shall have explained to you its import – that is to say, its full import. For it is like unto many of the prayers of men, in that it asks for more than he who utters it is aware of – except he pause and think."

"God's servant and yours has prayed his prayer. Has he paused and taken thought? Is it one prayer? No, it is two – one uttered, the other not. Both have reached the ear of Him Who heareth all supplications, the spoken and the unspoken. Ponder this – keep it in mind. If you would beseech a blessing upon yourself, beware! lest without intent you invoke a curse upon a neighbor at the same time. If you pray for the blessing of rain upon your crop which needs it, by that act you are possibly praying for a curse upon some neighbor's crop which may not need rain and can be injured by it."

"You have heard your servant's prayer – the uttered part of it. I am commissioned of God to put into words the other part of it – that part which the pastor – and also you in your hearts – fervently prayed silently. And ignorantly and unthinkingly? God grant that it was so! You heard these words: 'Grant us the victory, O Lord our God!' That is sufficient. *the whole* of the uttered prayer is compact into those pregnant words. Elaborations were not necessary. When you have prayed for victory you have prayed for many unmentioned results which follow victory – must follow it, cannot help but follow it. Upon the listening spirit of God fell also the unspoken part of the prayer. He commandeth me to put it into words. Listen!"

"O Lord our Father, our young patriots, idols of our hearts, go forth to battle – be Thou near them! With them – in spirit – we also go forth from the sweet peace of our beloved firesides to smite the foe. O Lord our God, help us to tear their soldiers to bloody shreds with our shells; help us to cover their smiling fields with the pale forms of their patriot dead; help us to drown the thunder of the guns with the shrieks of their wounded, writhing in pain; help us to lay waste their humble homes with a hurricane of fire; help us to wring the hearts of their unoffending widows with unavailing grief; help us to turn them out roofless with little children to wander unfriended the wastes of their desolated land in rags and hunger and thirst, sports of the sun flames of summer and the icy winds of winter, broken in spirit, worn with travail, imploring Thee for the refuge of the grave and denied it – for our sakes who adore Thee, Lord, blast their hopes, blight their lives, protract their bitter pilgrimage, make heavy their steps, water their way with their tears, stain the white snow with the blood of their wounded feet! We ask it, in the spirit of love, of Him Who is the Source of Love, and Who is the ever-faithful refuge and friend of all that are sore beset and seek His aid with humble and contrite hearts. Amen."

(After a pause.) "Ye have prayed it; if ye still desire it, speak! The messenger of the Most High waits!"

It was believed afterward that the man was a lunatic, because there was no sense in what he said.

And the Great War was a tragedy in that it prepared the way not only for part two of the world war, but as Strachan writes, "The First World War ... triggered the Russian Revolution and provided the bedrock for the Soviet Union ..."

"It laid the seeds for the conflict in the Middle East ... In short it shaped not just Europe but the world of the twentieth century."

But that first 'Christmas' shaped the daily lives of multitudes in all walks of life, in all the centuries thereafter.

To a discouraged band of those who, in that first century, followed Jesus, his birth came to what seemed the end – his death on a cross. But the end of that beginning was the Resurrection. The end of that beginning was life for all who will receive Him.

In His death, He took *our* penalty. The reparations demanded of us were paid in full by Him.

How could this be?

In reflecting on that which we celebrate at Christmas, *The Incarnation of the Word of God*, St. Athanasius wrote, "For God is good – or rather, of all goodness He is the Fountainhead, and it is impossible for one who is good to be mean or grudging about anything ..."

Speaking of God's mercy to us as His creation which bears His image, Athanasius goes on, "... it was our sorry case that caused the Word to come down, our transgression that called out His love for us, so that He made haste to help us ..."

"For when we were yet without strength, in due time Christ died for the ungodly ... God commends his love toward us in that, while we were yet sinners, Christ died for us ... For if, when we were enemies, we were reconciled to God by the death of his Son, much more, being reconciled, we shall be saved by his life."

Romans 5

Here rests the root of the peace of Christmas, peace with God who has had mercy on us, who has done for us what we could never do for ourselves.

This is the peace of which the shepherds heard.

"Glory to God in the highest and on earth, peace, goodwill toward men."

"Therefore being justified by faith, we have peace with God through our Lord Jesus Christ."

This peace offer still stands today. In the final invitation of the New Testament, it is offered to all:

I Jesus have sent mine angel to testify unto you these things in the churches. I am the root and the offspring of David, and the bright and morning star.

And the Spirit and the bride say, Come. And let him that heareth say, Come. And let him that is athirst come. And whosoever will, let him take the water of life freely.

... Everyone who hears this should say, "Come!" If you are thirsty, come! If you want life-giving water, come and take it. It's free!

... Whoever is thirsty, let him come; and whoever wishes, let him take the free gift of the water of life.

Epilogue

Isaiah 9

*T**he people that walked in darkness have seen a great light: they that dwell in the land of the shadow of death, upon them hath the light shined.*

Thou hast multiplied the nation, and not increased the joy: they joy before thee according to the joy in harvest, and as men rejoice when they divide the spoil.

For thou hast broken the yoke of his burden, and the staff of his shoulder, the rod of his oppressor, as in the day of Midian.

For every battle of the warrior is with confused noise, and garments rolled in blood; but this shall be with burning and fuel of fire. [see Note]

For unto us a child is born, unto us a son is given: and the government shall be upon his shoulder: and his name shall be called Wonderful Counsellor, The mighty God, The everlasting Father, The Prince of Peace.

Of the increase of his government and peace there shall be no end, upon the throne of David, and upon his kingdom, to order it, and to establish it with judgment and with justice from henceforth even for ever. The zeal of the LORD of hosts will perform this

OUR FATHER

which art in heaven,
Hallowed be thy name.
Thy kingdom come, Thy will be done
In earth, as it is in heaven.

Give us this day our daily bread,
And forgive us our debts,
as we forgive our debtors.
And lead us not into temptation,
But deliver us from evil.

For thine is the kingdom,
and the power and the glory, for ever.
Amen.

Note: "How will the Lord put an end to oppression? By putting an end to the warfare upon which oppression rests. God will not supplant oppression with greater oppression, nor will he replace warfare with warfare. Instead, he will do away with wars ... The boots whose tread shook the earth are now silent. The cloaks in whose fabric is mixed the blood of conqueror and conquered now feed the flames ...

There will be joy *because* God has delivered from oppression ... But how will he do *that*? This verse *'For unto us a child is born ...'* supplies the answer. It lies in the coming of a person ...", John N. Oswalt, *The Book of Isaiah*, NICOT.

Notes

The Christmas Letters of 1914 were transcribed by Operation Plum Pudding's volunteers. Unabridged and additional letters with the newspaper sources of this project may be found at *christmastruce.co.uk* on the world wide web.

Other letters may be found at *worldwar1.com*, including the unabridged description of Christmas Eve in the trenches by Henry Williamson. See especially the letters of Lt. West for a clear and touching account of what these men endured.

The account of the **6ᵗʰ Btn, The Gordon Highlanders** may be found at *kinnethmont.co.uk/1914-1918_files/xmas-truce.htm*

Pope Benedict XV's Peace Note may be found at *firstworldwar.com/source/papalpeacenote.htm*

MICHAEL C. SNOW is a fifth-generation family farmer. A graduate of the University of South Dakota, he served three years as an officer in the Marine Corps and nine years as a seasonal employee with the National Park Service. He earned his M.Div. at Earlham.

His writings have been published in several denominational magazines. Requests for his tract, "Your Child and Your TV" came from every state and from abroad. Elisabeth Elliot featured it as the format of one of her radio programs.

This is his third book.

For more information, please visit the author's website: *www.mikesnow.org*